CLASSIC
MOCKTAILS

The table of

CONTENTS

OUR CONCEPT

Step into the enchanting world of the "Classic Mocktail Recipe Book," where we present a meticulously curated collection of 50 exquisite non-alcoholic elixirs. This compilation is a celebration of the art of mixology without the need for spirits. Within these pages, you'll discover an array of timeless mocktails, from fruity fusions to herb-infused marvels, each meticulously crafted to redefine the boundaries of non-alcoholic beverages.

Whether you're hosting a lively gathering, enjoying a cozy night in, or seeking a refreshing pick-me-up during a midday pause, the "Classic Mocktail Recipe Book" promises a perfect solution for every occasion. Each recipe is an invitation to embark on a journey of flavor, health-conscious choices, and the sheer joy of mindful drinking.

Join us in exploring the myriad possibilities of mocktail creation, where every sip is a testament to the sophistication and creativity that can be achieved without the use of spirits. From exotic ingredients to unique garnishes, this book goes beyond mere recipes—it's an exploration of a lifestyle that celebrates the richness of non-alcoholic beverages.

So, here's to sipping and savoring the timeless magic of classic mocktails. Cheers to crafting beverages that transcend expectations and redefine the art of raising a glass in style!

MOJITO MOCKTAILS

Dive into the Mocktail Mojitos section of the "Classic Mocktail Recipe Book" and experience the vibrant fusion of tradition and innovation. Our carefully crafted recipes reimagine the classic mojito, infusing it with a burst of fresh flavors and tantalizing twists. From zesty citrus blends to herb-infused wonders, these mocktail mojitos promise to transport your taste buds to a realm of refreshing sophistication. Shake off the ordinary and embrace the extraordinary with our collection that proves you don't need alcohol to enjoy the essence of a classic mojito. Get ready to sip, savor, and elevate your mocktail game!!

Classic Mint Mojito

INGREDIENTS

20	fresh mint leaves
2	limes (juiced)
4 tbs	simple syrup
2	cups club soda
	Ice

DIRECTION

Muddle mint leaves with lime juice and simple syrup.

Add ice, club soda, and lime slices.

Stir gently.

GARNISH

Mint sprig and lime wedge

SERVING	CALLORIES	GLASS TYPE
4	~30	Highball glass

Watermelon Mint Mojito

INGREDIENTS

2 cups	fresh watermelon cubes
20	mint leaves
4 tbsp	honey
2 cups	watermelon juice
1 cup	soda water
	ice cubes

DIRECTION

Muddle watermelon cubes with mint leaves and honey.

Add ice, watermelon juice, and soda water.

Stir well.

GARNISH

Watermelon wedge and mint sprig

SERVING	CALLORIES	GLASS TYPE
4	~40	Highball glass

Apple Cinnamon Mojito

INGREDIENTS

2	apple slices
1 tbsp	ground cinnamon
1 tbsp	brown sugar
2 cups	apple juice
1 cup	sparkling cider
	ice cubes

DIRECTION

Muddle apple slices with cinnamon and brown sugar.

Add ice, apple juice, and sparkling cider.

Stir gently.

GARNISH

Apple slice, mint leaves, and a cinnamon stick

SERVING	CALLORIES	GLASS TYPE
4	~40	Mason jar

Cucumber Mint Mojito

INGREDIENTS

1	cucumber, thinly sliced
20	mint leaves
4 tbs	agave nectar
1 cups	cucumber-infused water
1 cups	club soda
	Ice cubes

DIRECTION

Muddle cucumber slices with mint leaves and agave nectar.

Add ice, cucumber water, and club soda.
Stir well.

GARNISH

Cucumber wheels and mint leaves

SERVING	CALLORIES	GLASS TYPE
4	~35	Rocks glass

Minty Blueberry Mojito

INGREDIENTS

1 cup	blueberries
20	mint leaves
4 tbsp	honey
2 cups	blueberry-infused water
2 cup	club soda
	ice cubes

DIRECTION

Muddle blueberries with mint leaves and honey.

Add ice, blueberry-infused water, and club soda.
Stir gently.

GARNISH

Blueberries and mint sprig

SERVING	CALLORIES	GLASS TYPE
4	~40	Collins glass

Ginger Citrus Mojito

INGREDIENTS

2 inch	fresh ginger (sliced)
2	limes (juiced)
1	orange (juiced)
2 tbsp	honey
2 cups	sparkling water
	ice cubes

DIRECTION

Muddle ginger slices with lime and orange juice.

Add ice, sparkling water, and a splash of orange zest.

Stir gently.

GARNISH

Lime wheel and mint leaves

SERVING	CALLORIES	GLASS TYPE
4	~50	Highball glass

Peach Passion Mojito

INGREDIENTS

2	peach slices
20	mint leaves
4 tbsp	maple syrup
2 cups	peach nectar
1 cup	passion fruit juice
	ice cubes

DIRECTION

Muddle peach slices with mint leaves and maple syrup.

Add ice, peach nectar, and passion fruit juice.

Stir well.

GARNISH

Peach slice and mint sprig

SERVING	CALLORIES	GLASS TYPE
4	~45	Rocks glass

Hibiscus Ginger Mojito

INGREDIENTS

2	hibiscus tea bags
20	mint leaves
4 tbsp	honey
2 cups	watermelon juice
1 cup	soda water
	ice cubes

DIRECTION

Steep hibiscus tea with ginger slices.

Cool, then mix with lime juice and agave syrup.

Add ice and top with ginger beer.

Stir gently.

GARNISH

Hibiscus flower and mint leaves

SERVING	CALLORIES	GLASS TYPE
4	~40	Mason jar

Lavender Lemon Mojito

INGREDIENTS

4 tbsp	lavender-infused simple syrup
2	lemons juiced
2 cups	soda water
	ice cubes

DIRECTION

SInfuse lavender into simple syrup.

Mix with lemon juice and soda water.

Add ice and stir gently.

GARNISH

Mint leaves

SERVING	CALLORIES	GLASS TYPE
4	~30	Rocks glass

Mango Tango Mojito

INGREDIENTS

1 cup	ripe mango chunks
2	limes (juiced)
4 tbsp	agave syrup
2 cups	mango nectar
1 cup	sparkling water
	ice cubes

DIRECTION

Muddle ripe mango chunks with lime juice and agave syrup.

Add ice, mango nectar, and sparkling water.

Stir well.

GARNISH

Mango chunks on a skewer, lime wheel and mint leaves

SERVING	CALLORIES	GLASS TYPE
4	~55	Rocks glass

Raspberry Rose Mojito

INGREDIENTS

1 cup	raspberries
1 tbsp	rosewater
4 tbsp	simple syrup
2 cups	raspberry-infused water
1 cup	soda water
	ice cubes

DIRECTION

Muddle raspberries with rosewater and simple syrup.

Add ice, raspberry-infused water, and soda water.

Stir gently.

GARNISH

Raspberries and a mint sprig

SERVING	CALLORIES	GLASS TYPE
4	~35	Rocks glass

Citrus Mint Mojito

INGREDIENTS

1	orange (sliced)
1	grapefruit (sliced)
1	lemon (sliced)
20	mint leaves
4 tbsp	agave nectar
2 cups	lemon soda water
1 cup	grapefruit soda water
	ice cubes

DIRECTION

Muddle a mix of citrus slices (orange, grapefruit, lemon) with mint leaves and agave nectar.

Add ice, and soda water.

Stir gently.

GARNISH

Citrus wheels and mint sprig

SERVING	CALLORIES	GLASS TYPE
4	~50	Collins glass

Blackberry Basil Mojito

INGREDIENTS

1 cup	blackberries
20	basil leaves
4 tbsp	maple syrup
2 cups	blackberry juice
1 cup	tonic water
	ice cubes

DIRECTION

Muddle blackberries with basil leaves and maple syrup.

Add ice, blackberry juice, and tonic water.

Stir well.

GARNISH

Blackberry and basil leaf garnish

SERVING	CALLORIES	GLASS TYPE
4	~45	Rocks glass

MULE MOCKTAILS

In the Mocktail Mules section of the "Classic Mocktail Recipe Book," we shake up tradition with a twist on the iconic mule. Explore our refreshing concoctions that replace the kick of alcohol with a burst of bold and effervescent flavors. From ginger-infused delights to fruit-forward marvels, these mocktail mules redefine the art of mule-making without a drop of spirits. Sip your way through this collection and discover that the zing without the sting is just as satisfying. Get ready to enjoy the lively spirit of a mule, alcohol-free and full of zest!

Cranberry Rosemary Mule

INGREDIENTS

2 cup	cranberry juice
2	limes (juiced)
4 tbsp	rosemary-infused simple syrup
2 cups	ginger beer
	ice cubes

DIRECTION

Mix cranberry juice, lime juice, and rosemary-infused simple syrup.

Add ice and top with ginger beer.

Stir well.

GARNISH

Cranberries, lime wedge and rosemary sprig

SERVING	CALLORIES	GLASS TYPE
4	~45	Copper mug

Citrus Ginger Mule

INGREDIENTS

1 cup	orange juice
2	limes (juiced)
4 tbsp	ginger syrup
2 cups	ginger beer
	ice cubes

DIRECTION

Mix orange juice, lime juice, and ginger syrup.

Add ice and top with ginger beer.

Stir gently.

GARNISH

Orange wheel and ginger slice

SERVING	CALLORIES	GLASS TYPE
4	~40	Copper mug

Cucumber Elderflower Mule

INGREDIENTS

1	cucumber (thinly sliced)
4 tbsp	elderflower syrup
2	limes (juiced)
3 cups	ginger beer
	ice cubes

DIRECTION

Muddle cucumber slices with elderflower syrup.

Mix with lime juice and ginger beer.

Add ice and stir well.

GARNISH

Cucumber wheels

SERVING	CALLORIES	GLASS TYPE
4	~40	Copper mug

Pineapple Mint Mule

INGREDIENTS

1 cup	pineapple chunks
20	mint leaves
1 cup	pineapple juice
2	limes (juiced)
4 tbsp	agave syrup
2 cups	club soda
	ice cubes

DIRECTION

Muddle pineapple chunks with mint leaves.

Mix with pineapple juice, lime juice, and agave syrup.

Add ice and top with club soda. Stir well.

GARNISH

Pineapple wedge, lime wedge and mint sprig

SERVING	CALLORIES	GLASS TYPE
4	~45	Copper mug

Raspberry Rose Mule

INGREDIENTS

1 cup	raspberries
1 tbsp	rosewater
4 tbsp	simple syrup
2	limes (juiced)
1 cup	raspberry juice
2 cup	ginger beer
	ice cubes

DIRECTION

Muddle raspberries with rosewater and simple syrup.

Mix with raspberry juice, lime juice, and ginger beer.

Add ice and stir gently.

GARNISH

Raspberry and lime skewer and a mint sprig

SERVING	CALLORIES	GLASS TYPE
4	~50	Copper mug

Mango Jalapeño Mule

INGREDIENTS

1 cup	mango chunks
8	jalapeño wheels
1 cup	mango nectar
2	limes (juiced)
4 tbsp	agave syrup
2 cups	ginger beer
	ice cubes

DIRECTION

Muddle mango chunks with 4 jalapeño wheels.

Mix with mango nectar, lime juice, and agave syrup.

Add ice and top with ginger beer.

Stir gently.

GARNISH

Jalapeño wheels and lime wedge

SERVING	CALLORIES	GLASS TYPE
4	~55	Copper mug

Blueberry Basil Mule

INGREDIENTS

1 cup	blueberries
20	basil leaves
4 tbsp	simple syrup
2	limes (juiced)
1 cup	blueberry juice
2 cups	ginger beer
	ice cubes

DIRECTION

Muddle blueberries with basil leaves and simple syrup.

Mix with blueberry juice, lime juice, and ginger beer.

Add ice and stir gently.

GARNISH

Blueberries and basil sprig

SERVING	CALLORIES	GLASS TYPE
4	~50	Copper mug

Apple Cinnamon Mule

INGREDIENTS

1 cup	apple juice
2	limes (juiced)
4 tbsp	cinnamon-infused simple syrup
2 cups	ginger beer
	ice cubes

DIRECTION

Mix apple juice, lime juice, and cinnamon-infused simple syrup.

Add ice and top with ginger beer.

Stir well.

GARNISH

Apple slice and cinnamon stick

SERVING	CALLORIES	GLASS TYPE
4	~40	Copper mug

Passionfruit Ginger Mule

INGREDIENTS

1 cup	blueberries
20	mint leaves
4 tbsp	agave syrup
2	limes (juiced)
2 cups	blueberry juice
2 cups	ginger beer
	ice cubes

DIRECTION

Mix passion fruit puree with lime juice and ginger syrup.

Add ice and top with ginger beer.

Stir gently.

GARNISH

Passion fruit seeds

SERVING	CALLORIES	GLASS TYPE
4	~55	Copper mug

Watermelon Basil Mule

INGREDIENTS

2 cups	watermelon cubes
20	basil leaves
2	limes (juiced)
4 tbsp	agave syrup
1 cup	watermelon juice
1 cups	club soda
	ice cubes

DIRECTION

Muddle watermelon cubes with basil leaves.

Mix with watermelon juice, lime juice, and agave syrup.

Add ice and top with ginger beer.

Stir well.

GARNISH

Watermelon wedge, lime wheel, and basil sprig

SERVING	CALLORIES	GLASS TYPE
4	~50	Copper mug

Blackberry Basil Mule

INGREDIENTS

1 cup	blackberries
20	basil leaves
1 cup	blackberry juice
2	limes (juiced)
4 tbsp	simple syrup
2 cups	ginger beer
	ice cubes

DIRECTION

Muddle blackberries with basil leaves and simple syrup.

Mix with blackberry juice, lime juice, and ginger beer.

Add ice and stir gently.

GARNISH

Blackberry, lime wedge and basil leaf garnish

SERVING	CALLORIES	GLASS TYPE
4	~50	Copper mug

Guava Lime Basil Mule

INGREDIENTS

1 cup	guava chunks
20	basil leaves
4 tbsp	honey
2	limes (juiced)
2 cups	guava nectar
2 cups	ginger beer
	ice cubes

DIRECTION

Muddle guava chunks with basil leaves and honey.

Mix with guava nectar, lime juice, and ginger beer.

Add ice and stir well.

GARNISH

Basil sprig

SERVING	CALLORIES	GLASS TYPE
4	~55	Copper mug

Mango Mint Mule

INGREDIENTS

1 cup	mango chunks
20	mint leaves
4 tbsp	simple syrup
2	2 limes (juiced)
1 cup	mango nectar
2 cups	ginger beer
	ice cubes

DIRECTION

Muddle mango chunks with mint leaves and simple syrup.

Mix with mango nectar, lime juice, and ginger beer.

Add ice and stir gently.

GARNISH

Mango chunks on skewer, lime wheels and mint sprig

SERVING	CALLORIES	GLASS TYPE
4	~50	Copper mug

Minted Blueberry Mule

INGREDIENTS

1 cup	blueberries
20	mint leaves
1 cups	blueberry juice
2	limes (juiced)
4 tbsp	agave syrup
2 cups	ginger beer
	ice cubes

DIRECTION

Muddle blueberries with mint leaves and agave syrup.

Mix with blueberry juice, lime juice, and ginger beer.

Add ice and stir gently.

GARNISH

Blueberries, lime wedge and mint sprig

SERVING	CALLORIES	GLASS TYPE
4	~50	Copper mug

Strawberry Mint Mule

INGREDIENTS

1 cup	strawberries
20	mint leaves
1 cup	strawberry juice
2	limes (juiced)
4 tbsp	simple syrup
2 cups	ginger beer
	ice cubes

DIRECTION

Muddle strawberries with mint leaves and simple syrup.

Mix with strawberry juice, lime juice, and ginger beer.

Add ice and stir gently.

GARNISH

Strawberry and mint sprig

SERVING	CALLORIES	GLASS TYPE
4	~45	Copper mug

SPRITZER MOCKTAILS

Indulge in effervescent elegance with the Mocktail Spritzers section of the "Classic Mocktail Recipe Book." Elevate your senses with a symphony of sparkling concoctions that bring together vibrant flavors and a touch of finesse. From berry-infused delights to herbaceous wonders, these mocktail spritzers are a celebration of bubbles, balance, and alcohol-free brilliance. Discover the art of crafting refreshing, sophisticated beverages that sparkle in both taste and presentation. Cheers to effervescence without compromise!

Citrus Berry Spritzer

INGREDIENTS

1 cup	mixed berry juice
1	lime (juiced)
1	lemon (juiced)
2 cups	sparkling water
	ice cubes

DIRECTION

Mix mixed berry juice with a splash of lime and lemon juice.

Add sparkling water and ice.

Stir gently.

GARNISH

Mixed berries on a skewer and mint leaves

SERVING	CALLORIES	GLASS TYPE
4	~35	Wine glass

Kiwi Mint Spritzer

INGREDIENTS

1	kiwis (peeled & sliced)
10	mint leaves
4 tbsp	agave syrup
2 cups	sparkling water
	ice cubes

DIRECTION

Blend kiwi with mint leaves and agave syrup.

Strain the mixture, add sparkling water, and ice.

Stir well.

GARNISH

Kiwi slices and mint sprig

SERVING	CALLORIES	GLASS TYPE
4	~40	Wine glass

Cran-Apple Rosemary Spritzer

INGREDIENTS

2 cups	cranberry juice
1 cup	apple juice
4 tbsp	rosemary-infused simple syrup
2 cups	sparkling water
	ice cubes

DIRECTION

Combine cranberry juice with apple juice and a hint of rosemary-infused simple syrup.

Add sparkling water, ice, and stir well.

GARNISH

Cranberries and rosemary sprig

SERVING	CALLORIES	GLASS TYPE
4	~50	Wine glass

Peach Basil Spritzer

INGREDIENTS

2	peaches (sliced)
20	basil leaves
4 tbsp	honey
1 cup	peach nectar
2 cups	sparkling water
	ice cubes

DIRECTION

Muddle peach slices with basil leaves and honey.

Mix with peach nectar, sparkling water, and ice.

Stir gently.

GARNISH

Peach slice and basil sprig

SERVING	CALLORIES	GLASS TYPE
4	~45	Collins glass

Watermelon Cucumber Spritzer

INGREDIENTS

2 cups	watermelon chunks
1/2	cucumber sliced
1	lime (juiced)
2 cups	sparkling water
	ice cubes

DIRECTION

Blend watermelon with cucumber slices and a splash of lime juice.

Strain, add sparkling water and ice, and stir well.

GARNISH

Watermelon wedge, mint sprig and cucumber wheel

SERVING	CALLORIES	GLASS TYPE
4	~35	Wine glass

Raspberry Lemon Spritzer

INGREDIENTS

2 cup	raspberries
1	lemon (sliced)
4 tbsp	agave syrup
2 cups	raspberry-infused water
1 cup	sparkling water
	ice cubes

DIRECTION

Muddle raspberries with lemon slices and agave syrup.

Mix with raspberry-infused water, sparkling water, and ice.

Stir gently.

GARNISH

Raspberries and lemon wheel

SERVING	CALLORIES	GLASS TYPE
4	~40	Wine glass

Mango Ginger Spritzer

INGREDIENTS

2 cups   mango chunks

2 inch   fresh ginger (sliced)

1   lime (juiced)

2 cups   sparkling water

         ice cubes

DIRECTION

Blend mango chunks with ginger slices and a splash of lime juice.

Strain, add sparkling water, and ice.

Stir well.

GARNISH

Mango slice

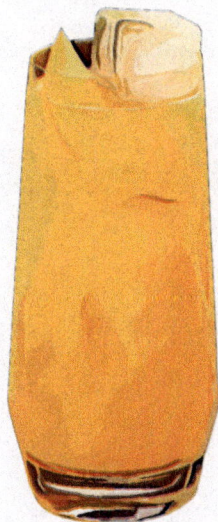

SERVING	CALLORIES	GLASS TYPE
4	~45	Collins glass

Mango Ginger Spritzer

INGREDIENTS

1 cup	blueberries
20	basil leaves
4 tbsp	simple syrup
2 cups	blueberry-infused water
1 cup	sparkling water
	ice cubes

DIRECTION

Muddle blueberries with basil leaves and simple syrup.

Mix with blueberry-infused water, sparkling water, and ice.

Stir gently.

GARNISH

Blueberries on a skewer and basil sprig

SERVING	CALLORIES	GLASS TYPE
4	~45	Rocks glass

Ginger Peach Spritzer

INGREDIENTS

2	peaches (sliced)
2 inch	fresh ginger (sliced)
4 tbsp	honey
2 cups	peach nectar
1 cup	sparkling water
	ice cubes

DIRECTION

Muddle peach slices with ginger slices and honey.

Mix with peach nectar, sparkling water, and ice.

Stir well.

GARNISH

Peach slice

SERVING	CALLORIES	GLASS TYPE
4	~50	Highball glass

Lavender Lemonade Spritzer

INGREDIENTS

2 cups	lavender-infused lemonade
2 tbsp	elderflower syrup
2 cups	sparkling water
	ice cubes

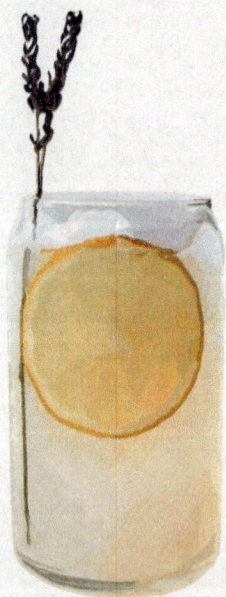

DIRECTION

Mix lavender-infused lemonade with a splash of elderflower syrup.

Add sparkling water, ice, and stir gently.

GARNISH

Lemon wheel and lavender sprig

SERVING	CALLORIES	GLASS TYPE
4	~35	Beer can glass

Minty Melon Spritzer

INGREDIENTS

2 cups	honeydew melon chunks
20	mint leaves
4 tbsp	agave syrup
1 cup	honeydew melon juice
2 cup	sparkling water
	ice cubes

DIRECTION

Muddle melon chunks with mint leaves and agave syrup.

Mix with melon juice, sparkling water, and ice.

Stir well.

GARNISH

Melon chunks and mint sprig

SERVING	CALLORIES	GLASS TYPE
4	~40	Wine glass

Strawberry Basil Spritzer

INGREDIENTS

1 cup	strawberries
20	basil leaves
4 tbsp	honey
2 cups	strawberry juice
1 cup	sparkling water
	ice cubes

DIRECTION

Muddle strawberries with basil leaves and honey.

Mix with strawberry juice, sparkling water, and ice.

Stir gently.

GARNISH

Strawberry and basil sprig

SERVING	CALLORIES	GLASS TYPE
4	~45	Wine glass

Peach Rosemary Spritzer

INGREDIENTS

2	peaches (sliced)
4 tbsp	rosemary-infused simple syrup
2 cups	peach nectar
1 cup	sparkling water
	ice cubes

DIRECTION

Muddle peach slices with rosemary-infused simple syrup.

Mix with peach nectar, sparkling water, and ice.

Stir well.

GARNISH

Peach slices and rosemary sprig

SERVING	CALLORIES	GLASS TYPE
4	~50	Collins glass

Citrus Mint Sparkler

INGREDIENTS

1 cup	mixed citrus juices (orange, grapefruit, lemon)
20	mint leaves
4 tbsp	agave syrup
2 cups	sparkling water
	ice cubes

DIRECTION

Mix a variety of citrus juices (orange, grapefruit, lemon) with mint leaves and agave syrup.

Add sparkling water, ice, and stir gently.

GARNISH

Citrus wheels and mint sprig

SERVING	CALLORIES	GLASS TYPE
4	~40	White wine glass

Pineapple Coconut Spritzer

INGREDIENTS

2 cups	pineapple juice
1 cup	coconut water
1	lime (juiced)
2 cups	sparkling water
	ice cubes

DIRECTION

Mix pineapple juice with coconut water and a splash of lime juice.

Add sparkling water, ice, and stir gently.

GARNISH

Pineapple wedge and Maraschino cherry

SERVING	CALLORIES	GLASS TYPE
4	~45	Wine glass

TONIC MOCKTAILS

Immerse yourself in the refreshing allure of the Mocktail Tonic section in the "Classic Mocktail Recipe Book." Our tonics redefine the art of revitalizing beverages, offering a symphony of flavors without a trace of alcohol. From herb-infused elixirs to fruit-forward tonics, each recipe is a crafted potion designed to invigorate your senses. Embrace the crisp, clean notes that characterize these mocktail tonics—a perfect accompaniment to any occasion. Get ready to experience the elixir of refreshment, sans the spirits, and savor the rejuvenating journey sip by sip!

Peach Basil Tonic

INGREDIENTS

2	peaches (sliced)
4 tbsp	agave syrup
20	basil leaves
2 cups	peach nectar
1 cup	tonic water
	ice cubes

DIRECTION

Muddle peach slices with basil leaves and agave syrup.

Mix with peach nectar, tonic water, and ice.

Stir gently.

GARNISH

Peach slices and basil sprig

SERVING	CALLORIES	GLASS TYPE
4	~45	Rocks glass

Watermelon Basil Tonic

INGREDIENTS

2 cups	watermelon cubes
20	basil leaves
4 tbsp	agave syrup
1 cup	watermelon juice
2 cups	tonic water
	ice cubes

DIRECTION

Muddle watermelon cubes with basil leaves and agave syrup.

Mix with watermelon juice, tonic water, and ice.

Stir well.

GARNISH

Watermelon wedge and basil sprig

SERVING	CALLORIES	GLASS TYPE
4	~40	Rocks glass

Ginger Pear Tonic

INGREDIENTS

2	pears (sliced)
2 inch	fresh ginger (sliced)
4 tbsp	honey
1 cup	pear nectar
2 cups	tonic water
	ice cubes

DIRECTION

Muddle pear slices with ginger slices and honey.

Mix with pear nectar, tonic water, and ice.

Stir gently.

GARNISH

Pear slice

SERVING	CALLORIES	GLASS TYPE
4	~40	Wine glass

Hibiscus Mint Tonic

INGREDIENTS

2	*hibiscus tea bags*
20	*ming leaves*
4 tbsp	*simple syrup*
1 cups	*tonic water*
	ice cubes

DIRECTION

Steep hibiscus tea with mint leaves in one cup of water.

Cool, then mix with simple syrup and tonic water.

Add ice and stir gently.

GARNISH

Mint sprig

SERVING	CALLORIES	GLASS TYPE
4	~35	Wine glass

Apple Cinnamon Tonic

INGREDIENTS

1 cup	apple juice
4 tbsp	cinnamon-infused simple syrup
20	basil leaves
2 cups	tonic water
	ice cubes

DIRECTION

Mix apple juice with cinnamon-infused simple syrup and tonic water.

Add ice and stir gently.

GARNISH

Apple slices and cinnamon sticks

SERVING	CALLORIES	GLASS TYPE
4	~35	Rocks glass

Cucumber Lime Tonic

INGREDIENTS

1	cucumber (thinly sliced)
2	limes (juiced)
4 tbsp	agave nectar
1 cup	cucumber-infused water
2 cups	tonic water
	ice cubes

DIRECTION

Muddle cucumber slices with lime juice and agave nectar.

Mix with cucumber-infused water, tonic water, and ice.

Stir well.

GARNISH

Cucumber wheel and lime wheel

SERVING	CALLORIES	GLASS TYPE
4	~35	Wine glass

Pineapple Mint Tonic

INGREDIENTS

1 cup	fresh pineapple chunks
20	mint leaves
4 tbsp	coconut sugar
1 cup	pineapple juice
2 cups	tonic water
	ice cubes

DIRECTION

Muddle pineapple chunks with mint leaves and coconut sugar.

Mix with pineapple juice, tonic water, and ice.

Stir gently.

GARNISH

Pineapple wedge, lime wedge, and mint sprig

SERVING	CALLORIES	GLASS TYPE
4	~45	Wine glass

Lavender Lemon Tonic

INGREDIENTS

2	lemons (juiced)
4 tbsp	lavender-infused simple syrup
2 cups	tonic water
	ice cubes

DIRECTION

Infuse lavender into simple syrup.

Mix with freshly squeezed lemon juice and tonic water.

Add ice and stir well.

GARNISH

Lemon wheels and lavender sprig

SERVING	CALLORIES	GLASS TYPE
4	~30	Rocks glass

Berry Rose Tonic

INGREDIENTS

1 cup	mixed berries
1 tbsp	rosewater
4 tbsp	simple syrup
1 cup	berry-infused water
2 cups	tonic water
	ice cubes

DIRECTION

Muddle mixed berries with rosewater and simple syrup.

Mix with berry-infused water, tonic water, and ice.

Stir well.

GARNISH

Rose petal

SERVING	CALLORIES	GLASS TYPE
4	~40	Rocks glass

Blueberry Basil Tonic

INGREDIENTS

1 cup	blueberries
4 tbsp	honey
10	basil leaves
2 cups	tonic water
1 cup	blueberry-infused water
	ice cubes

DIRECTION

Muddle blueberries with basil leaves and simple syrup.

Mix with blueberry-infused water, tonic water, and ice.

Stir gently.

GARNISH

Blueberries and basil sprig

SERVING	CALLORIES	GLASS TYPE
4	~45	Wine glass

Mango Jalapeño Tonic

INGREDIENTS

1 cup	mango chunks
8	jalapeño wheels
2	limes (juiced)
2 cups	tonic water
1 cup	mango nectar
	ice cubes

DIRECTION

Muddle mango chunks with jalapeño wheels.

Mix with mango nectar, lime juice, tonic water, and ice.

Stir gently.

GARNISH

Mango pieces on a skewer and lime wheels

SERVING	CALLORIES	GLASS TYPE
4	~55	Wine glass

Raspberry Rose Tonic

INGREDIENTS

1 cup	raspberries
1 tsp	rosewater
4 tbsp	simple syrup
2 cups	tonic water
1 cup	raspberry juice
	ice cubes

DIRECTION

Muddle raspberries with rosewater and simple syrup.

Mix with raspberry juice, tonic water, and ice.

Stir well.

GARNISH

Raspberry skewer

SERVING	CALLORIES	GLASS TYPE
4	~50	Wine glass

Cranberry Orange Tonic

INGREDIENTS

1 cup	cranberry juice
1 cup	orange juice
4 tsp	ginger, grated
1 cup	tonic water
	ice cubes

DIRECTION

Mix cranberry juice with orange juice and a hint of ginger.

Add tonic water, ice, and stir gently.

GARNISH

Orange wedge

SERVING	CALLORIES	GLASS TYPE
4	~40	Rocks glass

INDEX

INDEX

INDEX

Printed in Great Britain
by Amazon